Dog Gone It

and other stories

Cookie Crumbles

cookie crumbles

DOG GONE IT
and other stories

Cookie Crumbles

e: Lizard69q@aol.com

Buddha Press
Niles, Illinois

cookie crumbles

.CONTENTS.

cookie crumbles

M.A.R.S.
(Martial Arts Resolution Services)

Excerpt [2712 AD]: The Last Days of Man, the End of Human Hegemony by Bot6633325T

Legend had it that at one time reproduction was the primary focus of sexual activity. In the modern world there was no linkage between sex and reproduction, as in the work of the ancient writer Huxley, Society determined who should be reproduced. The rate was targeted at slightly beyond replacement.

A hive–in classical terms, a city-state–was designed for extremely limited growth. Resources and space itself were incredibly difficult to obtain. The hive had to be completely self-sufficient, insofar as it was able; but trade for certain items was a necessity.

Warren Concord stood at his dresser methodically picking socks out of the laundry basket looking for their mates. When found he folded them together and put them in the sock drawer. He was robotic. He continued until the basket was empty. Occasionally glancing at the picture window, really a holographic display, he saw a small glade that quickly receded to forest. A pair of hyperactive squirrels gamboled about, presumably without any serious thoughts filling their minds.

This man was in the prime of his life. While he did not lead a physically challenging existence his daily trips to the gym for strength training left him trim and years younger biologically than his calendar age. He had olive skin with deep brown eyes and hair. He was worthy of a second look from anyone not sworn to celibacy.

His eyes scanned the room, searching out some other mindless action to perform. Finding none he moved to the couch. He picked up a book from the end table and riffled the pages but could not alight long enough to begin to read. The title was Brave New World; Warren had purchased it at a subbasement used bookshop around the corner from his apartment block the day before.

He made a great effort to block out the morbid reality that threatened to overwhelm him. Reading Huxley's prose, time passed, pages were read but not absorbed.

Warren tossed the book aside. He instantly regretted the action--books themselves were an anachronism--far too delicate to be thrown about, unlike a sturdy crystal hand screen. Warren sometimes felt himself to be an anachronism; he didn't quite fit into this modern world.

The picture window warbled, the squirrels et al scrambled and reformatted to a headshot of Gabriel. Warren looked up from his box of take-out. Chopsticks hung frozen at his mouth holding cold dripping Mongolian beef. Gabriel--even after that initial emotional rocket ride--still had that 'time stands still' effect on Warren. He had a vivid sense memory of how his hands felt pressing against Gabriel's waist from either side, the balls of his thumbs massaging the small of his back. Of how the two of them just fit together as though they were carved simultaneously from the same sculptor's marble block.

Gabriel's mouth moved but no sound came. His eyes were blue, with pale Nordic skin and features. His face was extremely animated. His glossy blond hair was longish but still above his collar. Warren was not in love with Gabriel--but he desperately wanted to be. If only he could come to trust the young man, a boy really. And that boy was so engaging and completely without guile. To call him an open book was redundant. At the moment it was not hard to see that he was angry. Warren felt bad but was determined to hold his ground.

Warren said "Sound".

"...a miserable excuse for a human being. Really. I've been calling you for days, DAYS! I know you're there, pick up. Please. Come on, I'm worried about you." Said Gabriel.

Warren said, "Open". And continued to speak.

"Gabriel--I'm not interested! Really. I'm not interested in chatting, talking, communicating, communing, being there, being here, making time, marking time, hooking up or any other kind of sex, up to and including fucking." Warren said.

"Can I come over?" asked Gabriel, empty bravado, certain that he'd be rebuffed.

"Are you deaf?"

"No--just persistent" said Gabriel, changing his tone and trying to be lighthearted though he did not feel in the least bit carefree. "Aaah, I'll bring dinner!"

Warren lifted and shook the box of take out without responding.

"All right -- dessert then!"

"What do you **want**?" Warren asked.

"To see you!"

"You're seeing me now…"

"Please Warren, you're acting quite peculiar. Let me sit down with you and talk about what's eating you up."

"All right…all right. Come over, but I'm not interested in any feel good crap. You understand? My number is up and I'm more than a little crazy."

"I understand! I'll be right there," said Gabriel.

"Joshua? It's Gabriel. Listen something has come up, last minute."

"Hmmm, let me guess, Boyfriend has decided he does want to see you? So Anna and I won't have you crying on our couch at three o'clock in the morning this weekend?"

"That's really cold Joshua, you know I think Warren is the one. He's the man I've been looking for all my life."

"Instead of canceling why don't you just bring him home for dinner? Anna would love to meet him."

"But not you?"

"Oh, I KNOW who he is. And I know what he is. He's old enough to be your father. I realize you have a huge hole in your life cause your Dad walked out on Mom when you were a kid but my

Dad died before I was born. I understand your pain…"

"Joshua, he's a good man, he makes me happy, why won't you give him a chance?"

"I only…"

"Oh never mind I'll call you later."

Joshua actually felt the connection rip away and it was painful because he felt such a failure as a surrogate parent. When their mother succumbed to brain cancer she'd said that he must now be both mother and father to young Gabriel that his little brother needed his full attention. And yet he found Anna.

Excerpt [2712 AD]: The Last Days of Man, the End of Human Hegemony by Bot6633325T

The populace did not appear to recognize that a state of war existed. People simply went about their business, shopping, working, and going to school as they did any other day. Yet the war was real. It was being broadcast daily – channel 100 carried it live.

NorEast was at war with Riverine, again. The thousand miles that separated the two cities were a wasteland of scorched earth and deadly microbes–rampant mutations. The land and sky of the Deadlands were absolutely quiet. It had been so for seven hundred years.

This war was about water. NorEast had plenty of poisoned water, but only Riverine had clean fresh water, it was surrounded by water--and the glaciers north of the city provided much more than it needed. Clean water was absolutely essential to the farms that formed the base of all the cities. Riverine had cut the flow of water and NorEast had declared war.

Gabriel put his hand on Warren's chest and tried to slip it under his unbuttoned shirt. Warren's hand shot up and immobilized Gabriel's wrist. Warren was adamant that he wasn't going to let his lust for Gabriel cloud his thinking. This was the most critical juncture of his life. The fact that it was completely out of his control did not lessen his certainty that he must find a way.

"I'm **not** in the mood." Said Warren. "Sit. Talk--if you must."

"Why are you in this state?" Gabriel asked bluntly as he gracefully settled onto the couch.

"Aren't you paying attention to the war?" Said Warren. "At all?"

"Well, no more than usual, should I be?"

"How long have we been together?"

"Almost six months."

"It's not your fault. I guess it just never came up. You see -- I'm in the Guard, that's the only reason I can afford this apartment...the amenities I have. I certainly couldn't support it on my income from writing. As a ranking Officer of the Guard I have duties and responsibilities," said Warren.

"But, but it's just a very complex video game, after all it's not real," said Gabriel.

"Listen to me, the reality is revealed at the end of the conflict simulation. You were probably a baby the last time a full-scale conflagration happened. The Riverine counteroffensive has breached our defensive line. No one expected that. Our forces are in retreat, close to disarray. We may be routed. There could be Riverine troops crashing through the walls of NorEast at any moment. We've never faced a disaster of this magnitude in my lifetime."

"But why should you be so overwrought? Even if we lose this campaign, what would it matter to you? You are a well-regarded writer, a worthwhile artist; your works have been produced for the stage. Surely you are SP-plus?" asked Gabriel.

Warren was pained to contemplate how someone as beautiful and quite goodhearted as Gabriel could go through life as a leaf floating from one gust of sweet air to the next, never really scraping the ground long enough to feel the damage of experience.

"Survivor Points and the dead pool apply only to civilians. Anyone in the Guard is completely at risk, at all times. If the battle is truly lost I may not survive. I may not **want** to survive," said Warren grimly.

For a moment Warren was lost in his mind's eye as he imagined himself being a prisoner deep in the bowels of Riverine. Warren's palms were covered in a cold sweat; he rubbed them against each other as they dripped.

"Stop it! I can't stand to hear you say that. Of course you want to survive!" The sound of Gabriel's voice finally pierced Warren's paralytic revelry. Gabriel was shaking, completely undone hearing the man he loves talking of his demise -- even if obliquely.

Warren, still in the grip of that awful vision now found himself feeling that he must comfort Gabriel. Stiffly at first, he held out his arms to Gabriel, who eagerly embraced him.

"Gabriel, please don't cry. I'm not really that bad off," lied Warren.

Gabriel sighed and tried to stifle his sobs, only to start again. Warren held him with Gabriel's head tucked into his chest. He remembered in detail the night they met. The cat and mouse game they played as Warren tried his best to deny the lust that this boy inspired at his first glance.

A patron had come to Warren with the idea of producing one of Warren's darkest novels as a musical comedy for the stage. He convinced Warren that the juxtaposition would be hilarious. Warren didn't really have an official role in the production but the director was a personal friend. He happened to visit the theater the day auditions for the chorus line were being held. Gabriel was in the wings waiting to go on. Jason, the director, was running the auditions himself, Warren settled into the aisle seat of the first row to watch.

Jason called for the next audition and Gabriel took the stage with the utmost grace and confidence. He was shoeless, wearing black leggings, snug but not overly tight, but no shirt; instead he wore a vest with only the bottom two buttons done. It revealed his well-muscled arms and the top half of his sharp cut chest. He performed a languid dance routine to the spare beat of a set of bongo drums he'd recorded. He used a straight-backed chair as a partner.

Slinging it about, standing on it, flowing around it like a python, Gabriel was unbelievably fluid. Jason was entranced but Warren was dumbstruck.

As the drumbeat faded out, Jason said "You're in, see the stage manager for the details."

Warren walked up to Gabriel and started to introduce himself.

"Hi, I'm War..."

"I know who you are, it's a great pleasure to meet you!" Said Gabriel. "I've read everything you've ever produced. I'm a huge fan. I can't believe I'm going to be in a production that you've written."

"Well actually I didn't work up the treatment they going to use for the stage play. Musical comedy, that's not quite my strong suit."

"Don't be so modest, I'm sure you could write anything!" Said the star struck boy.

"Modesty has nothing to do with it. I am simply well aware of my own limitations. But I do appreciate your flattery and the absolutely charming way you deliver it," he said with a broad smile.

"Please don't think I'm an empty-headed chorus boy. I may be pretty but I am educated. Well I'm sure there are areas where I could use a little more focus. I'm completely ignorant about Politics for instance. Bores me to tears, real ones."

"Don't be too hard on yourself, so are most Politicians!"

As much as Warren fought the urge to wine, dine and bed this young man it was a lost cause. Their playful repartee led to dinner, to a dance club and finally to Warren's wonderfully seductive two level apartment with it's large balcony opening onto the Central Atrium. Gabriel did not see his humble windowless flat for days.

Excerpt [2712 AD]: The Last Days of Man, the End of Human Hegemony by Bot6633325T

The great Hives of the North American continent looked as though they could stand against any and all assaults. The oldest of them was over a kilometer high and covered an enormous footprint of hundreds of square kilos. But it was an illusion. There was very little in the way of raw materials to be had, everything had to be reclaimed from the ruins of the long ago America. The cities were akin to butterflies in a tornado, they would not survive a serious conflict.

And so there had to be rules to control that conflict. In a negotiation that lasted over a generation all the major city-states hammered out what came to be known as "Valkyries Rules" A virtual war that had very real consequences. Wars in which every building, every citizen, every resource was modeled and in play for both sides. Every attack and counterattack was precisely projected and resolved. And the number of dead, wounded, and crippled was tallied.

This warfare eliminated the need to expand the habitat to house an increasing population, even a population that barely exceeds replacement will eventually outstrip it's resources. Valkyries Rules fixed that. And the very last negotiated agreement was the solution to maintaining the genetic diversity of the cities. Prisoners of war were routinely identified and exchanged.

While the war was virtual, the death and dismemberment was very real. War Day was the culmination of the conflict. Everyone who was involved or touched in any way by the simulated war as recorded by MARS was notified to be present on the Ellipse for the

Judgment of War Day or face summary termination. Thus equilibrium had been maintained for over 500 years of Valkyries Rules History.

"Please Gabriel! Stop crying. I'm sorry, I don't even know what I'm sorry for, But, I'm glad you persisted until I agreed to see you. You mean so much to me! You really do. And it's not just the sex or your splendid body…"

"It's not? Oh now I am offended!" His silly grin belied his words, as he took a proffered tissue to dab his beautiful eyes.

"You have a solid core of goodness that lights up like a beacon. I know what you have to give is so much more than I deserve and I say that because I simply can't let myself fall in love with you. You deserve the return of your love in the fullness with which it was given, no holding back."

"Oh Warren, whatever it is that's stopping you, we can work it out together. We can be happy."

"But that's just it. We can't. I'm a Captain in the Guard. My command, my officers and my troops did not hold back the Riverine assault. I reviewed the broadcast in detail and there is no way I will escape alive. I'm not going to promise you marriage when my life expectancy can be measured in days, hours maybe."

Gabriel kissed Warren, his arms around his neck, pulling himself upward slightly. As always he loved the scent that lingered in Warren's hair and on his skin. It was masculine but not unduly harsh or too spicy. Warren broke the kiss but made no move to dislodge the boy's arms. Their eyes spoke their sadness. Finally, summoning up a store of strength he hadn't realized he had, Gabriel unlaced his fingers and stepped away.

"Goodbye my love. I'll finish my tears at home. Please don't ever forget how much I love you." said Gabriel.

The apartment was silent. Warren could feel the absence of Gabriel and the bitter taste of his decision. He paced the living room and scanned all the channels. He went out to the balcony and stood high in the clean fresh air of the Central Atrium watching a few of the many colorful tropical birds that had been engineered for city living. Yet he could not distract himself. Eventually he went to bed.

Warren slept but not restfully; it was as if the hum and crackle of an energy field surrounded his prostrate body. His limbs and head were spastic in jerky little movements. In his dreamscape Warren walked up to the massive black stone pillar that would determine his fate. Faceless simulacra rolled across the surface of the rock. The whole of the rock was able to display images of the battles from any point in the war. The broadcast gave no indication of whom the individuals were, what unit they belonged to or any identifiable data. But the pillar knew. The cold rough stone knew. And it would soon render judgment.

Gabriel also tried to sleep, with no success. Uncharacteristically he called up his wall monitor to watch the news. Horrified, he saw the Special Bulletin on Channel 100.

"The Joint Armed Services Central Committee announced today that the war was over. All military personnel are urged to put their affairs in order before reporting at 0700. War Day will be executed the day after tomorrow." There was no announcer, just a frozen image of the City in silhouette.

Excerpt [2712 AD]: The Last Days of Man, the End of Human Hegemony by Bot6633325T

NorEast and Riverine could not be more opposed. Riverine was a theocracy, a strange amalgam of ancient Fundamentalist Christianity with an overlay of UFOlogy as Cargo Cult. There were awful consequences for even the most minor transgressions and truly serious offenses merited such horrendous punishment that Death himself would blanch.

NorEast was it's polar opposite; the most obvious example was that gay people enjoyed a position of trust and admiration in the forward-looking City of NorEast. Their contributions to the arts and sciences were highly valued by society as reflected in their annual SP awards.

It must be mentioned that this treatment was in the government's best interest. The birth rate among the gay population was significantly lower than in the heterosexual community. In NorEast once you were licensed to procreate the government stayed out of it. Thus NorEast was more than happy to promote gay life as patriotic and responsible.

In Riverine the Sky Father held the lightening and no one was allowed to live a life not consistent with Holy Scripture. And that scripture held that gay people were an abomination that required the utmost purification that only the literal scourge might provide. While the threads of leather crimped into metal shards scored the skin and the victims cried for mercy, the priests would pray for Holy Intervention. Their prayer was that Sky Father would allow the victim would live long enough, to suffer long enough to achieve redemption so that the soul would be freed in fiery absolution. For if he died before that moment of liberation, the depths of Hell would consume the condemned forever.

Gabriel was consumed by the mind fogging passion of his love. Sober reflection was not available. He was going to save Warren at any cost. His course of action was absolutely out of character. He moved quietly and deliberately. Warren had not removed Gabriel's retina print from the security module, so entering the apartment was not difficult. He came to stand over the sleeping form of his lover.

As he stood there he replayed part of the conversation he'd had with his brother the previous day. His sibling was the senior data administrator in the NorEast Environmental Stability System. He had a string of Information Technology degrees a meter long after his name.

"Gabriel, I don't think you are in your right mind. I'm not going to help you kill your self," Joshua said. "Not to mention putting myself at risk of going to prison."

"It's not a certainty that I'll die."

"That's a quibble and you know it," said Joshua.

"Let me worry about that. You always bragged you could crack any system and clean up after yourself so no one could ever tell."

"I still can, the cyberbots I've created are autonomous and squeaky clean."

"We've been arguing for hours, I have very little time left if I'm going to save his life!"

"Why do you care so much?" Asked Joshua for what seemed the millionth time.

"I love him but it's more than that. More like besotted. I know I will never achieve the kind of success I dreamed I would as a young boy. I'm very good but I will never be legendary. And this impulse is not completely altruistic; I do have an ego. I mean there is a chance I won't get killed but if I do -- I know he will miss me terribly and write the most eloquent hagiography about me."

"And mere fame is worth losing your life?"

"NO, but immortality is! Romeo and Juliet, Heloise and Abelard, unrequited love reverberates through the Ages. A thousand years from now people will talk about Warren and Gabriel."

"I can't do it, I can't. You're my brother, I love you as much as you love your man."

"He is worth saving Joshua. I love him and I can save him and I'm not about to stand by and let him die."

"I just don't..."

"If we were talking about Anna, your wife, the love of your life, would you save her? Would you hesitate even a second?"

The words had left Gabriel's mouth like a dagger and found their mark in Joshua's heart. The only answer was yes, he would save Anna. He could not deny his brother's understanding. More than that he knew if he denied Gabriel his help he'd still lose his brother. Gabriel would never forgive him if Warren died. It would become his fault; he would own that ever-present ache in Gabriel's heart, not the crazy war. And so he released a cyberbot that tracked down every single telegenetic flag in the system that pointed to Warren and flipped it to Gabriel and also the reverse. The golden image of the system would eventually reassert itself but not soon enough to interfere with the plan.

As if on a thick rubber cord stretched to it's maximum his mind snapped back to the present. Gabriel held the aerosol gun with the sleep shot at the ready. He put the barrel against Warren's neck, found the carotid artery and fired. He would not regain consciousness for hours, well past his appointment with the black stone.

At 0700 Gabriel stood on the summit of NorEast, a projection far above any inhabited floors. The wind was cold and insistent, stinging his eyes. They began to tear up. He felt as though he were on the roof of the world. It was quite unusual; a citizen had little or no reason to venture outside, except for today, War Day. A three hundred sixty degree view revealed only the utter blankness of the Deadlands. Gabriel and the other thousands who filled the great expanse from edge to edge were standing on a gigantic ellipse the center of which was a mammoth hole that seemed to extend down endlessly.

Far above the gaping emptiness floated an enormous black torus. Huge gold-veined white marble columns surmounted the torus at regular intervals. At the center of the torus tractor beams suspended an irregularly faced rough black stone monolith. This super structure was known as the Hall of Heroes.

Circling the monolith from top to bottom was a double spiral walkway. Each half was ringed in blue pulsing energy every meter. Gabriel made his way to the inner edge of the Ellipse. The staircase met the edge and swooped out to the black pillar. You could see the other walkway, the one going down, you could see the faces of the people but you could not touch them. The space between the energy rings was like marshmallow, you could push against it, it would yield briefly but the pushback grew exponentially with distance.

Gabriel eventually reached the top and stepped off. Walking across the stone's surface caused--unknown to Gabriel--a swirl of nanobots to detach from the stone and infiltrate his body. They tasted him, verified his identity, and resolved his category. Had his ID indicated he was a civilian they would have applied his SP score. A disposition flag was rendered and began broadcasting. The nanobots burrowed into their new host and went dormant.

Reaching the far side of the stone Gabriel stepped onto the descending walkway that sank into the abyss. He kept walking as the hole above his head grew smaller and smaller until he was in buried in total darkness except for the blue light of the pulsing rings. He had long ago lost sight of the person ahead of him on the stairs. It was disorienting to keep walking downwards in the darkness and now there was no sound, even the scuff of his feet had gone silent. Gabriel felt himself fall.

"Captain Concord...Captain Concord?"

The disembodied voice waited for acknowledgment from Gabriel who took a long moment to realize he was supposed to be Warren.

"Yes, I'm here."

Gabriel could not move, not even his head. All he could see was white light. He was terrified.

"Am I dead?"

"Not quite. Before we begin the process, the City wishes to express your fellow citizen's gratitude for your service."

"You're welcome, I guess. Ah, am I going to die?"

"Actually…no."

"Who are you? Why can't I see anything except the white light?"

"I'm a 'bot, humans are not suited for this type of work…it's better for you not to see too much."

"What happened?"

"It appears that you and your men took very heavy artillery fire, and then your position was overrun by the enemy. You were the only survivor. Unfortunately a shell practically landed on top of you and you lost your legs and a lot of your right arm."

At that news Gabriel screamed, while he could not feel anything, the horror of that news sent searing bolts of dread through his emotional heart. He was prepared to die for Warren, but this horror was beyond death.

"Captain, please calm yourself. I was describing the simulation, nothing real has happened yet. You have options, none of them very good but it is your decision."

"What options? I'm afraid I neglected the background information," said Gabriel.

"While NorEast is a republic, it is a signatory to the Valkyries Rules. Riverine is ruled by sadistic thugs--as a 'bot I think I am impartial enough to make that claim--and they rammed the "maiming clause" into the Rules, they want the results of any War to be ongoing in the enemy cities, to lower their productivity."

"I had no idea."

"NorEast and the other republics forced an amendment to the Maiming Clause…"

"What can I do, what can I do?"

"As I said, your options are not very palatable. You can choose the maiming, the City will see to your rehabilitation; obviously you would have severe limitations. You can choose death, we could see to that immediately if you wish. Finally you can choose Expulsion."

"Expulsion? Into the Deadlands? But that is just slightly longer death."

"Quite. But we would outfit you with a protective suit, a rebreather that will oxygenate your lungs for at least a week, possibly ten days and a weapon. I would recommend the solar-sonic pistol, absolutely devastating at ranges up to 100 meters, recharge to full in only 40 minutes."

"How long do I have to choose?"

"Oh take your time sir, you have a full sixty seconds."

Gabriel didn't need the whole minute. He gladly chose Expulsion, he would leave the City alive and in one piece, for how long, who knows? In no time at all he was standing in an airlock with his equipment in place and the 'bot, a shiny chrome sphere with tentacles, hovering at eye level.

"I'll leave you here sir. Oh, do polarize your visor; it's quite sunny today. Good luck."

"Thanks. I think I'll need it."

The 'bot floated off, the inner iris closed and the outer one opened and Gabriel stepped out bravely into the new world.

The door chime demanded attention. Warren was moving very slowly. He remembered going to sleep knowing that he was to report to the Ellipse for Judgment in the morning. If he actually slept through War Day it could be MPs at the door. That couldn't be good.

He didn't feel well. His head felt like someone had stuffed a balloon through his nose and blew it up. It was pushing his eyeballs out of his skull.

As the door slid open it revealed two men holding out their badges for his inspection.

"And you are?" Asked the cop with the mustache.

"Warren Concord."

"You want to try again?"

"What are you talking about? I'm Warren Concord!"

"Listen mac, according to our information Warren Concord was expelled from the City this morning, he's probably dead by now. That being the case, you're squatting in this prime real estate and we're here to help you on your way."

"I'm Warren Concord! You morons! There's been some mistake."

"I'd watch my tone sir. Why don't you look into my fone, try not to blink," said the cop without the mustache.

The cop studied the screen for a moment and turned away from Warren to confer with his partner.

"Put your hands behind your back sir. We're going to take you down to the station for a little chat, try to get this all straightened out."

"What?"

"According to DataTek, you are Gabriel Sarafino, only he's about twenty years younger than you look. This whole thing is starting to smell bad and we're going to let our lieutenant figure it out."

With that the cop clicked the cuffs shut and they were on their way to the precinct.

cookie crumbles

Fast Ride on the Zamboni

It was late Friday afternoon. The Blue Line L rattles its way through the southwest side of Chicago to the Harlem Avenue station. Frank Stubbs sits in the crowded car and stares out the window as the bungalows roll past. After dragging his exhausted body home from the factory he has little energy left for introspection, he gave no thought to another week of his life being exchanged as payment of another stack of bills.

Frank knew he was lucky; make that incredibly lucky. The unemployment rate was stuck at 35%. The economy continued trying to climb out of depression. But Joyce, his wife of 15 years, had a cousin, who had a guy who turned him on to an investment that had paid off huge. So huge it, along with the oil glut, killed Texas and left Chicago the center of beef production in the USA. "Nobody needed no more cows when you could grow Porterhouse in a vat" was the conventional wisdom of the guys who still ran things in the Windy City. And Chicago Beef was the best; taste, texture and cost combined, it was killer. Her cousin had put a lock on a job in assembly for Frank. It was a tough job, when the process finished you had to clean the giant vats until the stainless steel shone like a mirror.

In the family room Frank grabbed a beer from his dorm size fridge and wedged himself into his brown leatherette recliner in front of his screen waiting for the Hawks pre-game show to conclude. His ample belly provided a handy surface for his platter of hot wings that his son Joey dropped off on his way out the door. He devoured them at a pace he once thought might qualify him for serious competitive eating events but somewhere along the arc his life had described, his ambition seemed to have dissipated--just like his hair.

"Frank?"

Joyce shouted out his name, an interrogative that could have been interpreted as 'where are you, what are you doing' but Joyce knew exactly where Frank was and exactly what he was doing. That knowledge did not comfort her.

"I've got to go," she shouted from the front room.

"What?"

"You know what, tonight's the finals in the Tournament. We've got a chance to beat the champs. The girls are counting on me to have another of my perfect games. I can do it, too! I can feel it."

"I'm glad."

"Sarcasm doesn't become you," said Joyce.

"I'm totally sincere."

"You do remember it's Joey's last performance tonight, right?"

"But the Hawks…"

"Your son snags the lead in the Freshman Frolic and you can't find your way to one single performance?"

"Oh come on, I don't see you there either."

"The tourney was exactly the same nights as the play, if we'd lost the first or second round I would have been front and center for his show!"

"What play are they doing?" Frank asked, since he hadn't read the blurbs.

"It's a revival, his theater coach rewrote it as a full musical…"

"Like Oklahoma?"

"Like To Wong Foo, he's got the Swayze role. You know, we saw it at that retrospective, you wanted to see *Next of Kin* and I wanted to see *Ghost* and we ended up seeing *To Wong Foo, Thanks for Everything, Julie Newmar.*"

"Oh my God," said Frank thinking of what the guys at work would say if they heard Joey was playing a drag queen.

With Frank turning white, Joyce disappeared into the entry hall closet, banged around for a moment and emerged into the front room in the throes of a full-throated scream holding her open bowling ball bag in front of her.

"Where the hell is my ball? That miserable bitch Clemenza took my ball and substituted this piece of crap! I'm going to drag her down the lane by her phony blonde hair and feed her to the pinsetter!"

"Joyce calm down! You're gonna blow out your pacemaker. You'll find your ball, the other girls'll put a cigarette out in her eye if she don't cough it up. Just go already, you'll miss the first round of drinks. The free one."

"Yeah, I guess you're right. Wish me luck."

"You don't need it."

Joyce's exit was punctuated by the slam of the front door. Frank began to relax now that he was alone in the house. The mere thought of going upstairs looking for an appropriate outfit to wear to Joey's play left him breathless, he decided to put it off a bit. The drone of the talking heads on screen tugged Frank's eyelids down.

The incipient dream state roiled and pulsed and pixel by pixel recreated a night in the glory days, back in 2010 when the Hawks smashed every opponent on the their way to claiming the Stanley Cup. Frank was still a handsome young man then with a full head of thick wavy hair.

Frank and his brother Mike were at loose ends, each with a pocket full of payday cash. They found themselves walking down Madison Street just east of Des Plaines Avenue in Forest Park, a working class Chicago suburb with block after block of Irish pubs, sports bars and restaurants, some newly upscale. A blue-collar rock and roll bar dedicated to the Blackhawks was coming up on the right. Zamboni's was a rocking place most any night; but on Fridays there was karaoke, which was always fun to watch. Good or bad the singers delivered diversion.

The bar wasn't jammed but it was busy, there weren't two adjacent stools available at the bar. The brothers stood just inside the doors near the pool table momentarilym scoping out a productive location.

"Holy shit!" Exclaimed Mike, "look at the end of the bar, see those two faggots? What the fuck are they doing here?"

The two guys in question were unaware of their effect on Mike.

Though one was somewhat older and taller than the other; he always passed for ten years younger. He wore multiple earrings in each ear and had a bleach blonde buzz cut. He was ordering another round of drinks. His companion was very cute and slender with dark spiky hair. He was engaged in a lively conversation with a pretty girl seated on the bar stool next to him who was apparently very disappointed to hear he was indeed gay.

"I'm gonna go over there and…"

"What the hell is wrong with you Mike?" Interrupted Frank, grabbing his brother's arm and dragging him back. "Who cares if they're gay? Christ sake, it's 2010, grow up."

The answer to Mike's question would have been unsatisfactory to anyone looking for a grand conspiracy. Gay infiltrators staking a claim on the sports bars on Madison Street was not in play. The truth was more mundane, the only remaining gay bar in town had been shutdown because it's liquor license was suspended. The two friends had been visiting straight bars that featured karaoke when the need to sing became overwhelming.

At that moment the karaoke DJ announced that Deak and Jimmy, the objects of Mike's scorn, were to take the stage in front of the giant Blackhawks logo to sing Summer Love. At the same time Frank had ordered two Leinenkugels from the bartender--after returning he handed one to Mike and took a long swig of his own.

"Look, your boyfriends are gonna sing, wanna join them?"

"Hey, fuck you Mikey, you dick."

"You wish."

Deak and Jimmy belted out their rendition of Summer Love staying pretty much in tune acquitting themselves honorably. Following Deak back to their spot, Jimmy slowed--he and Frank locked eyes. The crowd, as always, showed their love with a strong round of applause, the girl who'd been chatting Jimmy up all evening planted a bright red seal of approval on his right cheek.

"I appreciate the kiss but I'm still not taking the offer," Jimmy said, smiling.

"Can't blame a girl for trying."

"Not at all."

"Well, it looks like my Prince is not in the building," she said sliding off her stool, a brief shiver coursing down her spine to her stilettos. She picked up her silver beaded clutch, which matched her dress.

"See you next time?"

"Sure thing. Have a safe trip home."

Meanwhile Frank made a big show of taking his full pack of cigs out, smacking the filter end against the pool table rail, opening it and finally pulling one out and tucking it behind his ear. He fished his Zippo lighter out of his pocket, flicked it to see the spark and headed for the door.

A few seconds later, Jimmy said, "I'm going out for a smoke." Deak smiled.

A Google truck doing street level video recording would have seen Jimmy and Frank in a flat-out Hollywood clinch. Both boys wrapped so tight a neutrino couldn't have gotten between them.

Two cigarettes on the sidewalk smoldered with a hot red ash. Jimmy was thinking 'hmmm straight boy maybe, curious boy for sure', Frank was thinking 'my dick is so hard it hurts, what the fuck does that mean?' Jimmy was busy. His hands slipped down from the boy's shoulders to his waist. His left pulled Frank's belt away from his back and his right hand slipped inside the boy's pants like a snake hunting a meerkat in its den.

Jimmy decided against kissing him as he might get spooked and ruin the moment. So he slipped his educated tongue into Frank's left ear and gently caressed the outer folds while his hand occupied itself cupping half of a perfect bubble butt. His fingers traced the fine crack, the forefinger taking the lead between the pillows. Once he moistened the ear he blew a warm stream of air through tightly pursed lips; Jimmy's ministrations converted Frank into a giant cylinder battery. Electricity arced south pole to north and back again.

"Oh my god no one has ever touched me like that. How can you do that?" Said Frank in singular words separated by breaths taken and expelled all hurky jerky like.

"You've never been the object of a man's lust before, my sweet hot pepper boy."

Jimmy was holding Frank up as his knees were close to buckling, the strength beginning to drain from him as he started pulsing. Jimmy had plunged both his tongue and his fingertip into Frank's body. The boy let out a moan that vibrated wantonly at the base range of hearing. Just then a previously unnoticed passerby of the nosy Holy Roller persuasion took note of Jimmy's tongue in action.

"HEY, do you have your tongue in that's guy's ear?"

The magic moment shattered like a snow globe dropped from a viaduct. Frank's eyes snapped in the interloper's direction.

"YEAH I DO! What the fuck do you care?" Jimmy answered.

Surprised by the vehemence of the response the Roller started backing away.

"Ah, nothing, nothing at all," he said as he melted into blackness.

Frank stiffened up. Jimmy knew it was over.

"I gotta go, my brother could come out any second. Damn, I coulda…you could turn me gay, that's too crazy."

"It was nice, see you around," said Jimmy as he extricated himself from the situation.

The solidity of the dream dissolved like a broken shard of shaumtorte on the tongue.

Joey flitted about the kitchen, cleaning off the table, doing the dishes, taking out the garbage. His hair kept getting in his way so he took the scrunchy off his wrist and pulled it back in a ponytail. His hand brushed the dangle earrings he still wore as his character Vita in the play. He could see his dad snoring away in his recliner in the family room. When he had asked the stage manager if his father had picked up his ticket he was hurt but not surprised to learn he hadn't.

He was on a high so intense he dreaded waking in the morning back in the world where he didn't wear fabulous cocktail dresses to breakfast. The experience of inhabiting a different person on the stage, being free to explore places he couldn't go otherwise and getting positive feedback made him glow like he was a bundle of fiber optic glow sticks.

His character connected with the audience so deeply it was as if the overwhelming love expressed by all the women in that little town welled up inside him and he carried it away. He walked through the archway into the family room with it's crushing clutter of NASCAR, Blackhawks and Sox memorabilia, most of which was collected by his Mom and stood at his father's side. Even in jeans and T-shirt he was still Vita.

"Dad, wake up, Mom will be home soon," Joey said just touching his father's arm.

"Jimmy, don't go, I wanna talk to you!" Mumbled Frank.

"What?" Said Joey.

Frank came fully awake and saw Joey standing over him, not the chimera of his dream.

"Oh, sorry son, I must have been dreaming."

"Who is this Jimmy person?"

"Nobody, forget it."

"Why didn't you come to the Frolic tonight?"

"I'm sorry, I fell asleep watching TV, I'm really sorry, I wanted to be there, honestly. I was exhausted. I had a week from hell. This is gonna sound over the top but--we lost a guy in one of the vats."

"No shit? I'm never eating another CB steak again."

"We found him after we drained the vat, buried..."

"That is so disgusting."

"We threw out all the loins ya know," said Frank, "lost a shitload of money!"

"I'm so sure."

"Kee-rist, you got a smart mouth."

"Mom said you promised to clean up the kitchen, dishes and all."

"Oh man, what time is it? She'll have my ass if she comes home and it's not done."

"Don't worry, I took care of it. Even if you didn't come to see me."

"I'm sorry."

"Yeah, I know--like always, just remember you owe me."

"Hey Joey?"

"Yeah?"

"You missed some eyeliner."

"Oh, thanks Dad," he said with a twinkle in his eye.

Dog Gone It

A beautiful woman crowned with lustrous black hair lay unconscious on a wheeled table in a small room. There was a single window high off the ground. She had been sedated and restrained after she'd been found, unable to stand, on the inside of the Asylum's locked gate raging incoherently in various languages, none known to the doctors.

The Temple of Cybele was an unusual building, especially for a desert community. It was a copy of a sea shell but on a gargantuan scale. Two thirds of the way toward the back an altar stood where the priestess and her acolytes performed their rituals of life and love. Suspended from the arching roof was a second but much smaller shell, just the bottom piece, in it a statue of Cybele herself looked out over her faithful. A railing separated the altar area from the rest of the interior. No males or at least no uninitiated males were allowed beyond the railing.

Joseph came to love the Goddess as a young boy. Her mysteries excited his sense of awe as he contemplated the universe and all she had created. He grew to maturity, a strong handsome lad but without a patron, without prospects. He never had any money to offer during services but every Wednesday morning he would come to the Temple and scrub the floor stones on his hands and knees until they shone as clean as glass. This had been Joseph's weekly offering to the Goddess for a very long time. He hoped he was known to her.

"Your devotion to her glory is exemplary, my sisters often speak of you with affection."

Joseph's eyes rose from his work to the person addressing him. She was a vision of feminine perfection. Dark wavy hair fell almost to her waist and full firm breasts pushed out the bodice of her dress.

"Thank you, Priestess. I live for the Goddess."

"Oh no, I am not the Priestess, merely one of her acolytes. But you are most welcome. May I call you Joseph?"

"I would be honored."

"Well then, Joseph it shall be."

Gaea was well pleased with her creation, especially her creatures. She did insist on a certain distance between her and her faithful. Thus beyond the boundaries of paradise her name was the Living Goddess Cybele, but here at home, to her handmaidens and retainers she was simply Gaea.

She ambled leisurely through paradise luxuriating in the beauty of it all. Her thoughts turned to Michael and his young brother, her pet name for him was Fire. They were the culmination of her life's work, occupying a place somewhere between human and god. Creation and destruction, searching for perfection has been her ceaseless preoccupation for – how long? Being ageless does have its drawbacks. While her memory does encompass all, there is a certain effort, non-negligible, involved in dredging it up.

Michael and Fire were as far removed from humans as humans were from trees, yet all life shares some commonality, some spark. She was the be-all end-all and as such she had to always be on guard against losing perspective. The question, never far from her mind, was her sense of probity up to the task of being the overlord of all she surveyed? However that weighty question was brushed aside for the moment as a dog came bounding out of the woods onto the stone walkway; he sat down but kept his back completely erect. His large head with soulful brown eyes locked into Gaea's gaze.

"Speak Spectre, tell me you love me," she said laughing as she rubbed her knuckles on the top of the dog's massive head. His coat was the color of old adobe brick. He answered her with a series of deep yips that sounded so forlorn, a look of sadness swept across her face. She took a few steps off the path to pick up a short thick stick; she showed it to Spectre and threw it so high and far that it seemed to vanish.

"Go get it boy, bring it back to me."

The dog jumped to his feet and dashed off in a blur quicker than any flesh and blood animal had a right to do. Soon only a ripple through the tall grass showed his progress toward his task and then even that was gone.

After she had spent some time in meditation, perhaps hours, the sunlight waned and the windows of the palace began to glow from within. Fire came to find her; he stood before her, a glorious realization of her desire. Michael was pretty enough and as pleasant an interlude as she could ever want but Fire had something else, some edge that he brought of his own.

She reclined on a chaise and motioned Fire to her side. He sat and as she gestured with her left hand his robes fell away. He stretched out along side her and entered her. That space once occupied pulsed and was gone. They were fused.

"Ahhhh," she said. She put her hands to each side of his chest and then suddenly he lay on the couch and she was above him, floating. She reached out, put a finger to his breast and drew a small spiral outward. His skin, muscle and bones became transparent and his beating heart was rendered visible.

"My heart powers you and the universe," she said as he looked up at her with real fear rippling across his exquisite face.

Gaea held her right forefinger up then rested it above her left breast, as she pressed her own skin the finger tip sank into her body. Yet there was no seeping blood. When removed, the finger was covered in a golden glow which she spread across Fire's heart.

"You are sweeter than my most delicious honey," she said.

Fire never knew what to say in these encounters. While he suffered no pain – on the contrary – he felt a rush of well being quite apart from the orgasm that suffused his genitals. He remained silent apart from a single phrase.

"Thank you."

They lay together simply reveling in the after effects of the primal union they enjoyed. Fire while physically mature was – in the sense of real time – barely a year old, his existence in paradise was all he knew, his education not nearly complete.

Gaea's attention was roughly drawn away from her lover as Spectre bounded up, breathing hard, proudly holding the stick in his mouth. He sat, expectantly. She rose.

"Oh good boy!"

At her words he dropped the stick at her feet and moved forward to rub his back against her legs rumbling his pleasure at being this close to her. She lowered herself to reach his spine, stroking him vigorously. Spectre moved away, turned and fixed an imploring gaze on Gaea.

"No my dear, your time…has not yet come," she said to the dog and started her walk back to the palace.

Fire, naked, ignored, displaced by the dog, gathered his robes and slipped away.

"Michael, how is it that you never seem to chafe at the condition of our lives? We have everything and yet we own nothing. We have no work."

"I do…I am her eyes and ears. I observe the flows and eddies of the human torrent who love her. She depends on me to tell her what she needs to know," said Michael.

"I see," said Fire somewhat dubiously, "but all that is required of me is that I be beautiful? I want my life to count for something more than that."

"It does! Everyone knows you are her favorite. Though it does rankle me a bit since I am her first born. You, more than anyone, should be most satisfied. Has she ever denied you; said you couldn't do something, said you couldn't go somewhere?"

"No, not really, but then I've never asked."

"I'm sorry, I don't understand your dilemma. We serve her, we are her reflections," said Michael.

"I need more than that, I need purpose," said Fire.

"I feel unfulfilled. I know I have the capacity to achieve things more important than being an animated oil painting in your salon! I've read most of the books in your personal library, I hunger for more. Teach me! I was created in your image, let me amaze you."

"What do you want to know?" Gaea asked.

"Everything, every last bit of what you have learned over the many millennia."

"Fire! You simply don't deserve to know everything I know. I earned that right."

"Then what do you want from me? How can I prove I am worthy?"

"I don't know, your time is not my time. Have patience. There are cycles within cycles forever spinning; sometimes I think only to hear their own hum, the eternal nature of existence. You present me with a conundrum. How can I resolve it in a way that satisfies the both of us?" wondered Gaea aloud.

"What do you mean you're leaving?" Michael asked.

"Just that, I'm going into the world, I need to experience...the difference," said Fire.

"Have you told her?"

"No, I was hoping you would."

"Why?"

"I am afraid. I can't bear to see the slightest hint of disappointment in her eyes. I could never turn my back on her and walk away. I'm doomed."

"Hmmn, I think I agree with you."

The world was not at all what Fire expected. He thought it would be like life in paradise but a little less sophisticated, perhaps a little more rugged. He didn't expect that everything seemed covered in dirt. On the road Fire discovered something called coin of the realm and his lack of it. No coins? No food or drink or a dry place to sleep for that matter. He was determined not to fall back on asking someone at home for help.

After two more days on the road without encountering any other person he noted a figure approaching in the distance ahead. He was a big man, as hairy as a bear, as they came near he could see that the other man was more than a head taller than Fire, a lot more. He was carrying a sack slung over his shoulder as well as a short sword in a scabbard.

"Greetings," the hairy man said, "where are you heading?"

"Greetings to you, not quite sure where I'm headed. The nearest town I guess."

"That would be Three Palms; that is if you can call a blacksmithy, a tavern, a hotel and a garrison fort a town."

"How far is it?" asked Fire.

"About a day's walk."

"Guess I'll keep walking then."

"I'm going to get a fire going and cook up some dinner. You're welcome to join me."

"I don't want to be a bother."

"No bother at all."

"Thanks."

"Tell you what, you get the fire going while I find something tasty in the woods."

"Start the fire?" he said laughing.

"What's so funny? You know how, right?"

"Ah, it's just – my name is Fire – don't worry, I'll get it going."

"Oh, folks call me Ugly, I'll be right back."

"All right. Do you mind that they call you ugly? It's hurtful…and to be honest you don't look that bad."

"It's not how I look, it's what I do."

With that Ugly turned and ran off into the forest. Fire was disturbed by what he heard, but turned to the task at hand. Despite what Gaea called him, he did not know how to start a fire. He cleared a small circle of ground, found some tinder, some sticks and a few dry branches. Then he thought about how fire could be created.

Friction was key. He picked up a small stick as thick as his finger. He looked at his right hand intently and focused on his thumb and forefinger. He increased their density and surface tension geometrically then began to rub the length of the stick until it started to smoke; then a very small flame appeared. Fire gently blew on it, it grew more robust and he placed it in the center of the fuel he had prepared. It was a crackling mass of flames by the time Ugly returned with a fat rabbit in his hand.

The hunter twisted the head off the animal and quickly pulled the fur down until he was able to chop the feet off with his other weapon, a long wide heavy knife. After splitting the underside open he scraped out the body cavity with the blade.

"Stop gawking at me boy, never seen an animal field dressed before? Find some sticks for a spit, know what I need?" asked Ugly.

"Oh I do, I do."

Fire, feeling queasy, started looking around for the necessities. Shortly the former rabbit was browning nicely as Ugly turned the spit from time to time. The fat dripped into the hot coals creating snapping flames and a delicious scent of roasting meat surrounded the two mostly silent men. Other men smelled it too.

"Hey Sarge," said one of the Queen's Guard out on patrol returning to Three Palms, "Can you smell that meat cooking?"

"Yeah, it can't be far. Hope it's something big, eh?" said Sarge.

"Better hope they're the sharing kind," piped up one of the other troops.

The two of them ate the rabbit with gusto. Eating outside in the light of the lowering sun, fresh roasted animal, with your hands covered in grease and charcoal flecks is a primal experience, one that was unique for Fire. He found he liked it. They reclined on opposite sides of the fire.

"Wish I'd seen two of them, I'm still hungry," said Ugly.

"I know what you mean," said Fire all relaxed and kinda sleepy, flames dancing in his eyes.

"Now's as good as any time I figure," said Ugly.

"For what?"

"You ready to settle up?"

"What are you talking about?"

"I'm talking about what you owe me."

"I don't owe you anything."

"You ain't from around here, are you? The hunting, the cleaning, the cooking and the bunny. Ain't nothing free on the road. I figure you owe me at least one part of a gold sovereign, the economy being what it is and all."

The Queen's Guard came through the last degrees of a sweeping curve in the road rounding a copse of old growth trees. They saw two men standing over a campfire with a spit still upright. They couldn't make out the words from their distance but they could tell it wasn't a friendly chat.

"Damn, the meat's gone," said Sarge.

Ugly started circling the fire; he was enjoying the game, he didn't care if his dinner companion had money or not, he'd get his pound of flesh...

"Listen my friend, I have no money."

"Friend," he snorted, "what kind of fool goes down the road without any money in his purse?"

"I'm quite unfamiliar with this money business."

Now it was Ugly's turn to be astonished.

"In any case you owe me for dinner unless you want to end up like the rabbit."

"I don't have any of this money you want. And it's obvious to me this money is a bad thing, it's made you very unpleasant."

"Ugly?"

"Ahhh…"

"Listen my pretty young man, I'll take that ring you wear or the finger with it or maybe the whole hand, but you'll pay for my hospitality. Your choice."

Fire finally realized that Ugly meant to harm him, in a permanent way. On the next circuit of the guttering fire, the beast of a man picked up his weapons, sword in his right hand, and knife in his left.

"All right young master Fire, this is your last chance to give me what you owe me, my patience is at an end and I will not be deterred from settling your debt with blood."

"You're crazy; I'll be on my way now."

"That is not up to you," said Ugly.

The Guardsmen were close enough to hear the discussion now. The youngest trooper expressed the opinion that they should intervene; the laughter that greeted him convinced him of his error.

"What? Interrupt before the end of the show?" Queried Sarge, "not likely. You can't even buy entertainment in this forlorn billet and this is free! Pull up a seat gentlemen. Anyone want to take odds on the baby boy?"

No one wanted to cover his action.

"All right, I'll make it ten to one."

"I'll take that bet, for one part of a gold sovereign," said Sarge's second.

Ugly took a round house swing with the sword right at Fire's head. It never even came close. Over and over Fire implored Ugly to stand down. He refused and rained down blows with the sword and at the same time, on the comeback twist, tried to eviscerate Fire with his massive knife. The Guardsmen, all experts in close order hand to hand combat, stood amazed at the younger, smaller man's agility, being completely unarmed and, as yet, unscathed by Ugly's unbelievably virulent attack.

Fire repeatedly tried to leave the combat but Ugly would pursue him relentlessly. He could not turn his back on Ugly without running the risk of being skewered. Finally Fire stopped, feinted left, his opponent went right while Fire appeared to float above the ground just high enough to deliver a level blow of lethal power with his right fist directly into Ugly's heart. There was a very loud crack and the beast stopped short, inclined his head toward his foe, his eyes rolled up white in their sockets and he crashed to the ground, dead.

"By the Goddess, did you all see that? He killed him with a

single blow," said Sarge.

"I saw it all right, and I believe you owe me a gold sovereign," said the trooper who had made the bet with him.

The Guardsmen marched double-time over to the fire. Sarge was pretty sure he had recognized the aggressor, if so he was a wanted man, with a price on his head.

"Don't run off boy, we saw what you did, need to check a few things out," said Sarge.

"My experience of the last few hours makes me more than a little wary of strangers, please don't take offense."

"Don't worry; we're the Queen's Guard. You're in no danger from us. Besides, we saw you fight."

Ugly lay face down in the dirt. Fire unbuckled the dead man's leather harness, slipped it on himself, cinched it snug and rehung the sword and big knife. Sarge stepped up and rolled the corpse over with his foot.

"Well what do you know? You hit the jackpot boy, dependent on your taste in entertainment and victuals you've got a small fortune coming. This sack of meat is known as Ugly Jooba. The commander has sent out patrols to capture this guy for years and they always come back empty-handed or not at all."

"So what does that mean?" said Fire.

"It means you need to turn him in to the commander at the garrison in Three Palms. They're not going to take your word for it."

"I can't drag him all that way…"

Sarge threaded the fingers of his left hand through the tangled mess of Ugly's hair, pulling his head up off the ground.

"Let me see that sword for a second."

Fire took it out of the scabbard and handed it to the sergeant, hilt first. The trooper took it and neatly sliced the head off the body. Since he'd been dead for a while there was very little blood flow.

"Here," he said handing the trophy to Fire, "stick it in that bag he was carrying, you'll be able to haul it to the fort easy enough. You guys, drag the body into the woods, the scavengers will make short work of it. It's way too late to make Three Palms today, we need to sleep somewhere away from that fresh kill."

The troopers and Fire marched down the road until the night threatened to overtake twilight. They moved off the road a bit and settled in to sleep. The least senior guard made the fire, not too quickly either while Fire decided to keep his skill at that his secret.

"So a question if I might traveler, where did you learn to fight like that?" Sarge asked without waiting for permission to frame it.

"Learn? Well, I suppose you could say my mother taught me."

"Is that right? There is a legend that speaks of a Queen Hypolytta who rules over a place known as the Island Empire of the Eastern Ocean. If you believe in something as crazy as an ocean, who has ever seen that much water in one place? Anyway she allows no weapons of any kind and all her warriors are beautiful women who fight only with their bare hands. Sounds like your mother, maybe…"

"No I don't think so."

"Where do you come from then?"

"Ah, I come from Paradise, a very far place indeed. Please excuse me I've had a very hard day. Why don't we pick this up again in the morning?" said Fire eager to avoid talking about home.

"As you wish."

Dawn came and it was decided to move out with only hard biscuits for breakfast. Discussion of Fire's homeland did not resume as he fell back to the rear of the column with Sarge in the lead. The patrol moved fast and Fire shifted the cloth sack holding Ugly Jooba's head from shoulder to shoulder many times over the course of their march to Three Palms. But it still took the better part of a day to arrive at their destination. Sarge directed them straight to the commander's office at the fort.

"You will never guess what is in this bag sir," said Sarge standing at the commander's desk

"I'm too busy for games Sergeant, why don't you just tell me?"

He opened the bag and pulled Ugly out by his hair.

"What the...is that..."

"The one and only sir, Ugly Jooba himself."

"How did you and your boys get the drop on him?"

"Fire! Come up here," said Sarge.

The men moved aside to allow Fire to step forward to speak to the officer.

"My patrol had nothing to do with it. This civilian standing before you killed Jooba in hand-to-hand combat," said Sarge.

"I see. Any chance you'd like to join up boy? We could sure use a man like you."

"I appreciate the compliment sir but I am just passing through, no plans to settle down here, as interesting a place though it is."

"Then I won't hold you up, Sergeant, take this fellow to the Quartermaster and get him his reward," said the commander as he wrote out a requisition, "and get that filthy thing out of my office!"

"Sarge! How much did he get?"

"Like I expected, a small fortune, six gold Sovereigns, a year's pay for grunts like you and me. A word of advice Master giant killer?"

"Please," said Fire.

"Ask for your reward in silver marks, you don't want to be showing people gold, it's not healthy. If you don't mind my saying so you're a bit too naïve for the road," lectured Sarge.

The Quartermaster was very efficient. Fire and the Guardsmen were back outside as the sun began to sink below the horizon.

"Why don't you come with us for drinks? Me and the boys are plenty thirsty, we've been eating dust for a month," said Sarge.

"Well, maybe one."

"Come to think of it, you should be buying! If we hadn't shown up you would never have known you had it coming, think of it as a commission," said Sarge clapping Fire on the back.

"I guess that's true," he agreed.

One drink quickly turned into too many to count. The Guardsmen regaled each other and the rest of the tavern patrons, some of whom were also soldiers from other barracks within the fort, with stories of their various patrols. Out of deference to Fire's heroics they all refrained from talking about him and the end of Ugly Jooba, but they kept asking him to relate the events of the day and he continued to demur.

Finally after yet another prompting to relate his combat with Ugly, this time from a table across the room filled with soldiers, Fire relented and told his story. Possibly Fire was a better fighter than a raconteur as his tale fell rather flat.

"So let me get this story straight," said another sergeant sitting with his men at the opposite table, "the gist of it is he made dinner for you, he asked to borrow some money, you turned him down, he chased you around the fire with his sword and you got a lucky punch in and the old codger dropped dead. Don't sound like much of a big deal to me."

The crowd roared with laughter. Fire, having drunk more in this one sitting than the previous rest of his life stood up at his table and in the process knocked over his chair. The noise attracted the whole room's attention. In a tavern the sound of chairs scraping the floor ofttimes precedes the more silent snick of steel leaving the scabbard. In this case a lot of young men took to their feet, hands on hilts. The feeling of tension snapping strings of restraint washed over the barroom.

"Think what you want, I did not want to kill him…" said Fire.

"Maybe you'd want to show me your special fighting style," interrupted the troublemaker puffing out his chest.

"Oh shit," said Sarge coming back from the latrine into the scene of impending bloodletting.

The bar owner, having had more than one drunken brawl with soldiers destroying his livelihood knew exactly what to do

The tavern was well known for the pigs they raised in back of the building, the pens ran right up against the stockade wall of the fort. All the garbage and refuse produced by the tavern was dumped every night into the pens and the pigs cleaned it up. There were two suckling pigs on the spit in the huge fireplace, the scent of which had been drawing shouted questions of how much longer they had to wait to eat all evening.

"Olivia! Bring me all the flatbread in the kitchen and my favorite knife!"

With that said he hauled the table the young sergeant had stood up from across the room to the fireplace and pulled the pigs on to the almost clean surface, clean due to the puddles of beer. He started filling up the flatbread Olivia handed him with succulent smoky pork. They disappeared into the hands of hungry men as fast as they could be filled. All thoughts of fighting dissipated like the meat smoke itself.

By the time the pigs were a memory all the patrons had left except the two tables of Guardsmen, most of whom were unconscious.

Fire awoke to see his earlier antagonist taking young Olivia against her will. Her screams has roused him. She lay on the table next to the fireplace, in the grease and burnt pig crust with her skirts pushed up to her waist. She was fighting as hard as she could but she was no match for the bulging muscles of her attacker. The table itself however was. As he began to thrust, Olivia's struggles against him spun her off the slick table into the air.

Olivia's trajectory had much more lift than would otherwise have been expected. Fire lunged across the intervening space and caught Olivia in his arms. He set her into a chair and kissed her forehead.

"You're going to be all right child. He will never hurt you or any other woman again, I promise you."

She continued to cry, Fire's attempt to comfort her was halted by the impact of a shattering ceramic pitcher against his head wielded by the rapist.

"Do you want to die? What did they call you? Fire? She is a wench, she is nothing to me and even less to you. Why have you made me your enemy?"

"You are one of the Queen's Guard. She who rules in the name of the Goddess in Paradise and yet you choose to defile this woman, the Queen and the Goddess! I will not suffer the sound of your next breath," said Fire, become a coldly homicidal avenging angel.

"I look forward to proving you wrong," said the guardsman swinging his sword intent on taking Fire's head.

At this moment all the Guardsmen had been roused from their somnambulant states. To a man they were astounded by what they saw unfold before them. As the sword riffled the air scant inches from his unprotected neck, Fire reached out and grabbed it. Anyone versed in blade weapons would have expected his fingers to fly away but instead the hardened steel screeched and cracked into nuggets. At the same time Fire seemed to take on his namesake's power, light poured off his body, growing ever more intense. As the two combatants grappled the onlookers shielded their unbelieving eyes.

"If you have any faith in any God make your supplication now as you will meet them in the next instant," said Fire, as he twisted the head off his antagonist and threw it in the dying embers of the fireplace.

At the sight of the death of their compatriot all the soldiers in the room, save Sarge, threw themselves in full war cry atop Fire who fell to the floor under the crush of a dozen huge men who proceeded to slash, stab, and stomp him into the floor. They lived and died by their code, 'All for one and one for All'. Sarge went to Olivia, held her and turned her away from the annihilation of Fire. She could not stop shuddering.

Sarge was certain that his young friend was as dead as anyone could be. Despite the brevity of his association with him he felt a kinship that was undeniable. As disturbed as he was by this thought he was even more disturbed by the fact that he did not join in the attack on Fire. Why, for the first time in his career, had he failed to do his duty?

While the butchery was starting to slow down due to the muscle fatigue of Fire's assailants a small pulse of light erupted from beneath all the bodies. It continued to grow until a silent explosion of light as powerful as a volcano threw all the guardsmen crashing into the walls and ceiling of the barroom. When Sarge regained his sight Fire was standing in front of him, completely unmarked.

"Are you a God?" He asked.

"More than human, less than a God."

"Are they dead?"

"Yes."

"Could you bring them back before the boatman leaves?"

"Why?"

"They only did what they are trained to do."

"But not you?"

"I don't know why. What I am feeling at this moment is shame and yet relief at putting killing behind me. I could not participate in hurting you."

"See to it that the headless one is thrown to the pigs this night."

Fire pulled a small leather bag that held his remaining silver marks from inside his tunic and handed it to Sarge.

"Take this money and the girl away from this place, somewhere along the road you will find a Temple of Cybele, let her recover herself there. You might want to talk to the people you meet along the way about bringing the Living Goddess back into their lives. She seems almost forgotten here."

"I will."

"Since you won't be Sarge anymore what is your given name?"

"My mother called me Tarus."

"So be it. Take out the trash with you as you leave with your charge. You shouldn't be here when I return your good soldiers to this realm."

"Thank you."

"Fare well Tarus."

Fire eventually returned to paradise, but he no longer saw the perfection that he had experienced as an innocent. The air, the gardens, the colors all seemed slightly less now that he was aware of the imperfections of the world, how humans had to struggle and make sacrifice even to merely survive. He thought it could be better. For the very first time in his memory he thought his Mother might, no, must do better.

Fire held back in his intimate relations with Gaea, he had learned so much about both his body and his mind in the realm of the humans. He wanted her to let him in completely. To allow him to seep into every interstitial space and tissue that Gaea possessed. He was convinced that he needed to open his Mother's eyes to the inequities that existed in the world, disturbing things that he had witnessed in his travels. Beyond that he really didn't have a plan. He had the idea that by withdrawing, she would seek to entice him with greater, perhaps total access so he could give her the benefit of what he had learned.

Gaea's happiness at Fire's return was tempered by his unwillingness to return to her bed. She could force him, she could do anything she pleased but following such a path was beneath her. She set events in motion with an absolute determination not to interfere, no matter what the cost. He would come to her when he came to her.

The Goddess was at war within herself. She was patience incarnate but the perfection she had designed and built into Fire was something that she ached to experience again. The internal antipathy was of course that her superego felt her obsession with physical sexual pleasure was unworthy of her Godhead. She had no argument to oppose that indictment.

Fire's sojourn in the world had been the education that he had wanted from the Goddess but did not receive. He had made use of all the abilities that Gaea had given him in his mind's fully accessible areas, but more than that he was able to unlock those talents that Gaea had provided but buried for future use when she felt he was ready. He had exceeded her program.

He looked deeply into the infinity that was Gaea's soul, she was incredibly happy that he was able to complete her, this was why she created him, and he was fulfilling his destiny. Her normal defenses relaxed; she was rolling on huge waves of emotional satisfaction. He enveloped her; sealed her off and began to absorb her attributes, as much as he was able. He felt her, she became aware of his actions; in self protection she fled deeper into her core where she felt she would be safe. For the first time he was able to follow her in.

Gaea was beyond unconscious. She would not die, of that he was certain but she was extremely weak and would take time to recover, how much time he did not know. What he did know was that he had absorbed the manifestation of her core; that emanation he could integrate without harming himself as Gaea had used her own template when creating him. More than that he had managed to crystallize almost all her mystical core itself and transfer it into his own physical being. This action was incredibly dangerous as the Shard it formed would eventually burn through even his own godlike flesh.

Fire stood at the edge of paradise. He looked down, how far he had no idea; the surface was brown dotted with intense patches of green. He made a double fist and punched himself as hard as he could. He retched and felt something start moving up his throat, he pushed his left thumb and forefinger as far as he could into his mouth until he touched a slick faceted hard surface and was able to tug it out. It was almost nine inches long, green and crystalline. It was the essence of the Goddess. He had stolen it.

But he couldn't keep it. The Shard would not allow the unworthy to hold it. He knew the Shard wanted to return to her. It was already starting to get hot, he couldn't fathom what would happen next, he had assaulted Gaea herself, his Goddess, his creator. Could there be a greater crime? He began to go weak at his knees.

Fire held the Shard in his strong right hand; drew back his arm and threw it as far as he could. Even his preternaturally sighted eyes quickly lost track of the crystal as it fell back to the world. He felt himself losing his balance and then consciousness itself, he was spent.

When Fire came to he was in a panic, what if her attendants had found her body? He could lose his head over this. He rushed back to where he had seen her last. She was still laid out on the ground. While he was on his way the sun had dropped below the horizon. The aftermath of his attack on the Goddess had the cover of darkness. He needed a plan. Specifically, how could he transport Gaea's body without incurring any further damage and to where would he transport it? Time was running out. Then it came to him, the stables!

Fire threw a saddle on his favorite gryphon and grabbed a loop of rope off the stable wall, once outside they took to the air and landed next to Gaea. He used the rope to rig a harness so the gryphon could carry the Goddess' body. He decided to take her to a facility he knew about, an Asylum, which would have experience with people claiming to be god...they would know what to do with her. By the time he arrived it was the depths of the night, the gryphon landed within the gated compound. Fire untied the harness and stood over her still body.

"Gaea, my Goddess...I did the unthinkable, I committed virtual Deicide; but I had to, you've lost your way. You have to give the humans more direction; your 'hands off' policy is not fruitful. I had to take action. My only hope is that someday you will understand if not forgive me. I love you with all my being."

With that he swung back into his saddle and the massive wings of the gryphon lifted off into the moonless night.

Over many years the huge oasis that, through the centuries, drew both animals and humans to satisfy their thirst in the various springs that flowed ceaselessly came to be known as Old Town. It was abuzz in preparation for the coming of the planting season and with it the great Blessing of Seeds, the Initiate Procession was winding through the maze of streets culminating in the annual ceremony of induction at the Temple. Joseph had made a lifetime decision. His family had lived in their small apartment for many generations never amassing a surplus that would allow social ascendancy. Even if he never ate another meal he would never save a brideprice, he would die alone without progeny. He decided he was going to offer himself to Cybele as an Initiate. He hoped he would not dishonor his family by failing the trial. As the Procession passed where he stood he stepped into the mass of celebrants.

It was quite a sight, dozens of torch bearers, many many drummers, not to mention the players of cymbals and triangles adding their crashing notes to the din. As they approached the entrance to the Temple they danced between two solid walls of fire to the steps that led to the massive bronze doors now set open. The boisterous crowd filled the huge interior edge to edge.

The Priestess climbed the altar stairs to address the celebrants.

"Let those who have come tonight to give themselves to the Goddess step forward."

While the honor of joining the sisterhood of Cybele was legendary it was a good deal more difficult for a male than it was for a female. All a woman had to do was promise to remain chaste in thrall to the Goddess, males had to prove it. In the hours leading to the Temple many young men boasted of their devotion and their dedication to the Goddess and how they intended to secure their family's favor in the eyes of Cybele. But very few ever really made the final walk to the railing.

The three male initiates moved to the deeply grooved stone floor in front of the railing and knelt bowing their heads. Those who would serve her must be her reflections here on the physical realm. The Priestess took an obsidian blade from its place on the altar and handed it to the first kneeling figure. He untied his garment and let it fall behind him.

The young man pulled his testicles as far away from his body as he could and began to draw the volcanic glass blade through his scrotum from the underside. His forehead turned deathly white and sweat dripped down the sides of his face as his blood began to flow to the floor. But he could not complete the cut. The pain escaped his mouth in a scream that brought a burst of saliva to the mouth of every non-female in the Temple.

"Help me," he said as he fell unconscious against the railing.

The crowd had fallen silent. The Priestess pointed to two men standing nearest the failed initiate.

"Take him to the infirmary, hurry, and put pressure on his wound."

The second initiate took the blade from the hand of the Priestess and quickly disrobed. He appeared to be well prepared for the ceremony; he acted as though fully entranced. His movements were fluid yet precise. He handled the knife as though it were part of his arm with no hesitation or wasted motion. He pulled the sac away from his body until the skin was stretched as tight as a drum head. His eyes were focused on the Goddess; he never even glanced at what he was doing. In one quick yet unhurried motion he pulled the blade up and through, his testicles and surrounding skin came away clean. He dropped them and repeated the process for his penis, beginning the cut at the very base; it was over just as quickly as the first cut. Not a sound had passed his lips.

The priestess took the flat iron rod out of the red glowing brazier and quickly cauterized the wounds of the new acolyte still kneeling next to Joseph. The smell of burnt flesh filled the air of the Temple. She directed him to be removed to the infirmary. The Priestess picked the obsidian blade from the floor, wiped it clean of blood and ran the edge through the flames of the brazier. She handed it to Joseph. Already naked, he took the blade in his right hand and pulled his sac taut with his left. He took a deep breath and put the edge to his flesh. He began what he knew would be a very hard process.

The Priestess suddenly stiffened her spine and shouted out.

"Joseph! Stop. The Goddess commands it. She has a different

path for you to walk."

"What?"

Joseph was stunned and horribly shamed that he had been refused by the Goddess.

"The night of the initiates is complete. Everyone is to leave the Temple, except Joseph," she announced to the assembled worshippers, "you are to continue kneeling at the railing until Cybele has given you her counsel."

"I don't understand, have I displeased the Goddess in some way? I would gladly die to appease her."

"No, She is most pleased with you, and you may yet die to serve her."

"Her will be done." Joseph said.

Luci silently stole into Michael's suite, he was deeply asleep, breathing regularly. She constructed a tableau in her mind of Fire standing in this very room talking to Michael while holding her hand, telling him that he was leaving paradise to seek enlightenment. That the Goddess had elevated Luci from a handmaiden to her suzerain, Gaea's instrument. But more than that she injected the memory that Michael wanted Luci for his own consort. She moved closer to his head and leaned in until it was skin to skin and transferred that construct to Michael, and then she slid under the covers and lay beside him.

Luci made sure to wake before Michael. She put breakfast foods on a tray and took it into the bed chamber setting it on his night table. She awoke him with a passionate kiss.

"Good morning my darling, did you sleep well?"

Michael looked startled and confused for a moment and then the construct Luci had prepared functioned as designed and the shadow passed from his mien and he smiled broadly and answered.

"Yes, quite. You were a ravenous vixen last night. Thank you for that."

Standing in the formal gardens of the palace Luci gazed out at the cloud flecked blue sky. The warmth of the sun soaked into her outstretched bare arms. She pronounced it good.

She wore a diaphanous teal empire waist gown threaded with gold. It just cleared the flagstones that wound through the flowers and shrubs. Her sandals were white leather trimmed in gold with only a suggestion of a heel.

She walked toward the nearest stand of poplar trees meaning to find a place to sit in the shade while the running brook sang to her. She never tired of this diversion. Luci lowered herself to the ground without a care that she might stain her beautiful dress. She sat directly at the edge of the stream and trailed her fingertips, really only her long red nails, through the water. She flicked the drops up as she smiled. Each drop shimmered iridescently then unfolded into winged sprites that soared and gamboled about in the air each trying their best to amuse her

Her absolutely buoyant mood was soured though, brought crashing to the ground as Gaea's damn dog came splashing through the water, stopped in front of her and proceeded to shake off, completely soaking her delicate gown, leaving her quite exposed. In the past Luci would have swallowed her considerable annoyance since the dog was well favored by the powerful, but not this time.

"I want this beast transported out of my sight! But don't hurt it…I just never want to encounter it again."

While she didn't speak to anyone in particular she knew it would be done.

"Woof, woof…"

"What's that? What are you saying boy?"

"Woof!"

The dog continued his frenzied barking as he tore at the manicured grass at the edge of the sidewalk that ran the perimeter of the Asylum. The old man did not understand what the dog was trying to tell him. But Spectre was determined to enter the grounds, he felt a call that he was duty bound to answer. While Joseph had spent a life changing night in the forbidding building behind the massive stone walls, in the aftermath – like an iron door slamming shut – his memory was cut off.

The night in question was the time he, Joseph, had decided to give himself to the Goddess in the Spring Festival. After the Priestess told him to wait as long as it took for Cybele to make herself known to him the Temple fell silent and the only sound was the blood rushing through his inner ears and the hiss of the two burning tapers.

Joseph felt so lost, what could possibly be his fate, how would the Goddess choose to communicate with him? What could she possibly need from him? He became aware of a scraping noise coming from Cybele herself. Her stone head was rotating toward where he knelt.

"Do not be afraid. Let your heart be calm, you are under my protection, no harm can visit you. Come to me, I have need of you," said the statue of Cybele.

"Where, my Goddess, where shall I go?"

"Release your hold of your body, I will direct your energy, I will bring you to me. Do you trust in me?"

"With every breath I take."

Joseph felt extremely odd as his feet were animated by the Goddess, he started out at a fast walk but soon found himself running at a pace he could never have achieved on a normal day. He was simply a passenger in his own body. Joseph lost track of time but did recognize the forbidding gates of the Asylum that was surrounded by stone walls that looked insurmountable when he came to a stop before them. The gates were constructed of heavy iron bars, the gaps were far too narrow to allow Joseph to pass between them. In her weakened state the Goddess chose the more direct route, no time for finesse.

"Joseph, you must spread the bars apart, just enough to allow you to squeeze past."

"I don't think that I have the strength to do that."

"No, you don't so I will provide it."

Joseph did her bidding and as she said the bars simply deformed as he pressured them. He made his way to the main building, the door was locked.

"Now what?"

"Take the pins out of the hinges."

"I can't do that…"

"Have a little faith, my child."

It was the work of a moment and Joseph caught the door as it fell forward toward the steps. A few footfalls into the semi-dark interior and he encountered a man in a white coat holding a sheaf of papers.

"Oh my, how did you get out of your ward? Where are your clothes?"

Even though he was much taller Joseph's hands quickly found the doctor's throat and gently laid him on the floor, looking as though he had just fallen asleep.

"You might want to take his coat and papers."

"Will he be all right?"

"Of course, he'll awaken without even a memory of what happened."

Luckily there were no other encounters on their way to the room where Gaea was held. Her door was not even locked; the attendants felt the restraints were sufficient. Entering her cell Joseph was almost overcome with rage at the indignity done to his

Goddess. While he was not quite surprised by the fact that she looked completely human he did wonder how she came to be incapacitated.

"Joseph, you have more pressing concerns. Humans did not do this to me. I am in no danger. I will recover, in time. But you must play your part. Get up on the table, give me your seed."

He finally realized her voice was in his head, her physical body incapable of volition. Now he wondered if her Temple statue had actually moved? Naked again he pulled himself up onto the table, while this unconscious woman did not stir a muscle; her body did rise off the table until her extremities pulled her restraints tight.

Having nothing to compare the experience to he did not realize that as soon as he was erect enough to enter her, his sperm rushed into the woman as if drawn by an irresistible force.

"Oh Joseph you have given me a boy, a girl would have been more to my liking."

"I'm sorry Goddess."

"No mind, it will take me a thousand years to reclaim my essence, bit by savage bit, but I can build my warchild in mere weeks."

"What?"

"When he is finished crying into the world, one of my Daughters of Cybele will bring him to you and you will raise him, protect him, and keep him safe from Fire. Do you promise this to me?"

"Of course, I won't let him anywhere near fire."

Gaea was about to correct his misunderstanding when she thought better of it. If Fire found him and the baby they would both be erased. No sense in worrying Joseph unnecessarily.

"I will send you my most faithful companion, his name is Spectre; he will be instrumental at the proper time."

He did not remember how he left the cell, the Asylum itself or his journey back to his family abode, but he did arrive somewhat before dawn. His grandmother was preparing his breakfast.

"I didn't know you were already awake." She said not knowing he had only just returned home from the adventure of a lifetime.

"I'm not at all hungry, nana," he said, "but I am exhausted."

"Come here in the light, you look odd, you look ten years older than when I saw you last."

"Don't be silly. I'm exactly the same."

But his grandmother had been correct. In the days that followed his encounter with the Goddess, he watched the youth drain out of his face, his body. No human had the sum of resources to be expended with such abandon. Joseph had become prematurely old.

"Come along now boy," he said as he yanked on the dog's leash finally getting him to cooperate and move away from the gates.

Their walk back to the apartment was not terribly long. The dog was calmer but obviously anticipating the return of his young master. He would lie down on his favorite spot in front of the balcony doors where he loved to lounge in the heat of the desert day. He was a big well muscled animal with a large head, the color of weathered adobe, lean and supple. Running down one of the narrow streets in Old Town he would disappear as he passed the original mud brick buildings. In the apartment after a few moments he'd jump up, run to the door, yelp, look back at the old man and – seemingly – sigh then walk back to his spot.

Joseph had taught his son everything he knew about the world; after that he sent the boy to the market where he would sit at the feet of learned men engaging in argument and discussion. He would remember every word they said. And each night he would return to the apartment and tell Joseph what he had learned that day.

Years later Joseph asked Sonny what he was going to do with his life. Sonny was uncertain but said he felt restless, sometimes to the point of wanting to strike out blindly across the desert to find his destiny. This was something Joseph did not encourage, but he felt that one day it would have to come to pass. Joseph, trying to walk to the kitchen, was bowled over by Spectre chasing Sonny down the hallway.

"Sonny! How old are you?" Shouted Joseph to his son after regaining his feet.

"Seventeen."

"That is old enough to know better than to run rings around an old man like me. I'd likely die from a broken hip ya know? Take him outside and run all you want."

That would be the last time Joseph ever set eyes on his son.

"Yes Father, come along Spectre."

The boy and his dog played fetch in the street for a while, Sonny expected to wear Spectre out but at the point where he usually flopped down panting until Sonny brought him some water he got a second wind of epic proportions and took off running. The boy could not keep up with him. They traveled through one neighborhood after another getting more and more distant from their apartment. Eventually he found himself trekking over sand dunes out of sight of the streets and buildings calling to Spectre to stop running, but the dog would sit still waiting for him to approach and then take off running once again. Sonny was more annoyed with the dog than any other time he could remember.

Spectre was definitely slowing down. He was probably thirsty, the heat was punishing. Sonny caught up, wary of yet another sprint away in the wrong direction by the dog. He was panting now, looking extremely in need of water.

"Well boy, you've really gone and done it this time! We both need a drink, you more than me but where are we going to find any springs around here?"

Spectre trotted off through a narrow ravine between two series of towering dunes, loathe as he was to do it, Sonny followed. Once on the other side he was quite surprised. He saw a small encampment, three large tents and a corral holding horses, donkeys and camels. There were cooking fires and a canopy held up by four tethered poles, a beautiful woman lounged on a divan at a low table smoking from a hookah. Spectre ran up to her and licked her hand. She petted the dog on the head and spoke to Sonny.

"Welcome to my home young man, one might quibble over it being more of a camp, but it is my home none the less."

"Thank you."

"May I offer you and your animal water and food?"

"Please we could use both."

The woman rang a small bell and a man appeared at her elbow instantly.

"Please bring our guests food and water, would you like some beer as well?"

"Oh yes, that would be appreciated."

"We don't get many visitors but then we do move around rather frequently. How did you come to find us?"

"It wasn't my idea. My dog ran through the streets and alleys of Old Town until he was out of pavement, I thought he'd turn back but then he tore through the desert like he knew right where he was going. I wanted to abandon him a dozen times, the last time right over those dunes behind us. I followed him, determined that this time it was the last time, but then we discovered your encampment."

"But wasn't it already in your heart to explore the world, certainly more than the few twists and turns that bound your childhood home?"

"How do you know that?"

"You are of that age."

"Well, you are more correct than you know, Of late I have been feeling hemmed in, closed off, I'm a grown man; I should be making my way in the world, maybe set off on a quest, like a Hero in ancient times. But my knowledge of my own history is very incomplete. My father is a good man but he has never shared his story with me, when I ask him questions he often tells me that he doesn't remember. For instance I know nothing about my mother, nothing."

"I see. That must be very disturbing; you have to have a huge hole in your heart."

"Indeed I have to bury my concerns, since my questions only serve to upset my father and my grandmother. I've never been able to get any answers, it's a pointless exercise."

Her servant returned with the food and drink she requested. He put it on the table and backed away

"Before we share a meal we must introduce ourselves, my name is Espin Skya, I live the life of a nomad. I am a trader in antiquities, as was my mother and her mother before her. And you?"

"Nothing so grand I'm afraid. Just the poor son of my father, everyone calls me Sonny."

Espin poured two glasses of water from a carafe and handed one to Sonny. She took a sip from hers before she spoke.

"I have something of import to tell you. It could be the spark you need to change your life, to set you on the direction that you were meant to have. I want to tell you the story of the 'Dagger of God'."

"I would very much like to hear it, please tell me."

"There was a young woman whose father was involved in a business deal with a man who was a collector of all things exotic, people as well. This client's name was Zerxes. The father could not close the deal, he was a shrewd negotiator but he committed the cardinal sin of the trading life. His desire seeped out the pores of his skin in a scent of desperation. The other man, recognizing his weakness, kept upping the ante. Originally this man had offered the woman's father a considerable amount of money for his daughter. He, of course, refused to sell his daughter into slavery. But now, in his mind, he saw himself sinking into a morass of failure. His honor could not allow that. He felt if he could only make this deal he would cement a partnership that would bring him and his family untold wealth. And so he fell into Zerxes' trap. At the end he offered his daughter, for no recompense at all, to seal the transaction."

"How horrible! Did he come to his senses and stop it?" Asked Sonny.

"Oh no, his porters packed all the pieces for which Zerxes had bargained. Taking his daughter by the hand the three of them walked through the entrance of his tent and standing under the canopy he said goodbye to her. She would not raise her eyes to her father's face, it was just as well because in that very moment the heavy cloth of the canopy was rent, a green emerald like object, pointed at one end and rounded as a pommel at the other sank with a sickening thwack into the skull of her father. At that sound she looked up and their eyes spoke, she forgave him. He died at her feet."

"What happened? What did Zerxes do?"

"He tried to pull the dagger from the man's head. It did not budge, he had to brace his left foot on the corpse's shoulder and heave with both hands. It came away perfectly clean. Not a speck of blood or brain. He pushed the girl into the arms of his majordomo and told him to secure her. He put the dagger in an inner pocket of his robe and within minutes his caravan was back on the Great East Road."

"What happened to the girl, it was you, wasn't it?"

"Yes it was. Well, to be sure I was very afraid of what lay ahead but none of my fears materialized. It is said that no one can possess the 'Dagger of God' and remain alive unless that person lives only to return it to the living Goddess. Very soon chaos overtook Zerxes and his retainers left him and me behind."

"Where is the living Goddess?"

"That my young friend is for you to discover. It is my belief that you have been sent to me for instruction. You are to take up the great task, find the Green Dagger and return it to the Goddess."

"How do I even begin to search?"

"You have signposts to seek out. Each of the unworthy who coveted the great relic die, their skin takes on a sickly green cast that intensifies over a brief time until they match the emerald glow of the crystal dagger itself. The final pain they endure is terrifying to behold as their muscles become as hard as that which they covet so much. The last human thing they do is scream to the heavens as their throat crackles at the end of their metamorphosis."

"So I must follow the trail of human statues across the great desert until I find that last thief that has not yet succumbed to the curse? It sounds like a great adventure."

"Yes, it will be. Come into my tent, I will make it all clear to you."

Espin rose to her feet and in a colorful swirl of silks she led the way to her personal living quarters. The interior of her tent was elegant and sumptuous to both the eye and the hand. Treasures from every trade route traveled by caravan found their way to her pavilion. The center of the vast space was dominated by an irregular shaped thing covered by a tapestry of an elephant trumpeting to some unknown purpose. She took hold of one edge of the large needlepoint and spoke to Sonny as she quickly whipped it aside.

"Behold the emerald cast of the first possessor, Zerxes himself," said Espin.

He had been a large man. His face was raised skyward, the last moments of lucid thought plainly obvious to any observer. It was unpleasant in the extreme.

"So now you know what you are looking for!"

"I do, thank you," said Sonny, "it must give you a certain satisfaction to gaze upon him."

"Oh yes. More than you can imagine. You will sleep here tonight and tomorrow I will make you the gift of horses and supplies to speed you on your way."

Luci had come to know the price of stewardship. The seasons turned as regular as a prayer wheel, and despite the love and attention she lavished on her faithful it was never enough. At times her frustration with teaching the way to happiness sickened her. In the first days of her reign she often choked on the bile of her guilt. The image of her Mother lying comatose in the shaded meadow haunted her. As much as Luci tried to expunge it, it would worm its way back into her consciousness manifesting at first as a mere speck that would eventually metastasize into a throbbing presence she could not ignore.

Over the many years of her Regency, intimate familiarity with the sequence of events that led to Gaea being deposed – by her own hand – did not prevent Luci from re-imagining it as having been thrust upon her. It came to be not her doing at all as a matter of fact.

Her religious obligations and duties, while weighing heavily on her heart, were not the most troubling to her. That would be her relationship with Michael, who, even all these years later, still operated on the embedded premise that he was madly in thrall to his paramour Luci. She often thought about releasing him from his conditioning but recoiled from that action in fear of his probable righteous anger. She felt trapped. These days she avoided Michael as much as possible. His ever present love and generous solicitous behavior served only to make her cringe on the inside and when it slipped through her mask to be viewed by him; the look of pain that suffused his countenance was undeniable and more and more untenable.

Sonny did not know how many human statues marked the trail of the 'Dagger of God' but he had located many dozens of them over the years of his trek. This night, once more falling to sleep under the stars there was no hint in his mind that the morning would bring any new experience to his daily exercise of following the signs and portents in his pursuit.

But shortly after dawn it proved to be unlike all the preceding days of sand, sun and oasis. Spectre, as always, was running far ahead. He had run down the far side of a dune and now he scrambled back up and sat, head fully erect, keening a sound that had to mean 'hurry up as fast as that old nag can carry you'. When Sonny arrived, after urging his horse to her greatest effort, the reason was clearly visible at the bottom of the dune. A green man writhing in pain in the earliest stage of the great change. Without bothering to remount Sonny ran as fast as he could in sand sucking at his feet, halfway down he fell to his hands and knees and rolled the last dozen yards. Spectre managed, as always, to maintain his dignity.

"Where is it?" He shouted out after regaining his feet.

"Help me, oh Goddess help me! I have such awful pain," said the green man.

"I doubt that she can help you now. Especially since you were running away from her. Where is the Dagger?"

The dying man pulled the relic out of his boot and held it out; his arm froze in crystallization as he did so. Sonny gently took it from his hand, but the man's little finger still cracked and fell to the sand.

"It will be over soon," he said as he put his hand on the prone man's head in a gesture of comfort. And very soon it was.

Sonny had rawhide strips in his saddlebags and he proceeded to tie the Dagger in a leather lattice and attached it to a braid he wore around his neck. Afterward it never left contact with his chest.

The euphoria Sonny felt at having located the relic eventually slipped away on the long and tedious journey back to Old Town. He didn't even know why exactly he was going there. But deep in his heart it just felt like the right thing to do. Legend had it that no one could hold the Dagger for more than three days without dying if they weren't returning it to the Living Goddess so at least he knew he was heading in the right direction. Months had passed; he was still alive and not the slightest bit green. He was very glad to be going home for another reason; his father could not live forever. He needed to see him.

Olivia, the latest Priestess of Cybele the Living Goddess at Old Town, sat at Joseph's side and changed the cool compresses on his forehead as soon as they lost their effectiveness. She considered it a great honor to attend to him in his last days. She was the daughter of Cybele who had delivered the yowling baby to Joseph's care those thirty years before. When Joseph could no longer make his weekly walk to the Temple she had begun visiting him at home, she was very sad to see his steady deterioration. She knew the great favor with which he was regarded by the Goddess. It pained her that almost every day before she took her leave to attend to the Temple's business he would ask her if Sonny would come to see him today.

"Olivia, am I going to see Sonny today?" The effort to speak greatly taxed the old man.

"Oh Joseph, I would like nothing better than to tell you yes but I don't think it will come to pass."

"He must hurry. I will soon be gone on my own."

"I won't lie to you, it is so."

As their conversation wound down a strong knocking at the door commenced. Joseph tried to respond but Olivia put her finger to his lips and said she would go to the door. At her hand the door swung open and framed there stood a young man with lustrous dark hair to his shoulders, next to him a big silent dog the color of bricks.

"Greetings, is this still the home of Joseph?"

"Yes."

"I'm Sonny and this is Spectre."

"Yes, I remember you well. My name is Olivia; I brought you to this house shortly after you were born. It is fortuitous that you arrived today, you're father is dying. Come I will take you to him."

Sonny became distraught, he knew how long he'd been gone without a word passing between them. He hoped to receive his father's blessing even though he'd been such a disappointment as his son. Would Joseph understand Sonny's choices? As he stepped into his father's field of vision Sonny saw a change of expression suffuse the old man's face.

"Sonny! It's been so long. I can't believe what a man you have become. Come sit beside me so I can touch you and know for certain this is not just another fever dream."

"Father, I am so so sorry for having abandoned you. Believe me when I tell you it was never my intention to do so. My fate was ripped away from me, I found myself on a Holy Trek to serve the Living Goddess all the way to the far side of the great desert. But it is done now, I have what it is said belongs to her and her alone. My last task will be to return it to her or perhaps her representative here in this realm," he said with an acknowledgment of the Priestess.

Olivia had been hanging back trying not to intrude on this precious father and son reunion but Sonny's words reduced her good intentions to naught. She prayed she might know the answer without having to be so gauche as to ask.

"Sonny, there is no need for you to feel guilty, you served the Goddess like any other believer, her needs came first," said Joseph, "but what could you possibly have found that belonged to the immortal Goddess herself?"

"Father, have you ever heard the legend of the 'Dagger of God'?"

At these words the Priestess' eyebrows lifted off her forehead. She had always been sure this legend was as ephemeral as any other. To see concrete realization would be beyond anything she had experienced since her conversion to an acolyte of the Goddess that long ago night in a crossroads barroom. Sonny stood and unfastened his tunic at his left shoulder; it fell aside to reveal the green relic hanging from his neck.

"This object has killed untold numbers of men in a most horrific way, all of whom tried to possess it without the intent to return it to her. I have worn it nearest my heart for many months with no ill effect, it knows I wish only her will be done."

"Olivia, do you know this legend?" asked Joseph.

"I have heard it, I never gave it much credence," she answered.

"I assure you every word is true," said Sonny.

"I must return to the Temple. You two have much to say to each other that do not require a third pair of ears. Sonny it is wonderful to see you after all this time. My blessings on you. I'll see myself out."

Joseph surprised himself by a return of his appetite. He asked Sonny if he could prepare a meal for them to share, saying he would find what he needed for a healthy soup in the kitchen. A short while later Joseph felt strong enough to sit at the table; in fact he felt as if he was not sick at all. Where this crescendo of energy was coming from he could not say. Sonny ladled out soup with bread for their meal. When they finished Sonny prepared himself to ask a question that he had never received an acceptable answer to before. He hoped it would not debase an otherwise wonderful return to his father's house.

"Father, I hesitate to pose this query but I must."

"I have no secrets from you my son."

"That's good to know."

Sonny's face did not reveal his true reaction, disbelief, to his father's bold statement.

"I wish I could avoid this topic but your health concerns me. I need to know the answer that has eluded me all these years, who is my mother, when did she die?"

Whether self-induced or the result of external pressure the fog that to this point had always obscured the memory of Joseph's night that sired Sonny dissipated for the first time. Each detail stood in sharp edged relief including what the cost of those events was in terms of his lifespan. Joseph dreaded Sonny's reaction if he told him the absolute truth, he could not bear it if Sonny thought he was lying or worse that he was insane.

"Your mother is still alive, as to whether she could speak to you should you ever meet her I can not say. The one and only time I ever set eyes on her she was in a coma of sorts, unresponsive to questions yet it was said she was prone to extreme outbursts in tongues not known to anyone in attendance."

"But where is she?"

"At the Asylum. She has been there since before you were born."

"I want to see her."

"That is probably not possible."

"I will make it possible. Tell me where you last saw her."

"I will draw you a map."

Joseph and Sonny embraced, said their fare thee wells and the father watched his son walk away. He was unsure if he was right or wrong to deny him the knowledge that he was the son of the Goddess, but she could tell him herself, which would be all the proof needed. Joseph suddenly became very light headed; he braced himself against the back of a kitchen chair. It became overbalanced and he crashed to the floor, his last burst of life finally exhausted.

Michael and Luci were in the same room for a change. She seemed to be in a pleasant enough mood. That was very soon to change. Michael had recently been in communion with the various Temple Priestess', something he regularly did in order to help the faithful in times of dire circumstance. In this case a Priestess named Olivia asked him a question of theology that stunned him. She inquired as to the consequences of the return of the 'Dagger of God' to the possession of the Living Goddess. Michael was not even aware of the currency of this offshoot; some might call it heresy that had grown up in the last few decades. While those living in paradise were aware that Gaea had left in pursuit of her own agenda with Luci acting as Regent, no one in the human realm knew any such thing.

"Luci my dear, are you familiar with this thing called the

'Dagger of God'?"

"Hhhhmmm, I don't think I am, is it a real thing or a constellation, or what?"

"A Priestess named Olivia told me about it. She says she has seen it, it is quite real."

"Olivia?" said Luci, feeling very cold in her core suddenly.

"Do you know her?"

"No, I couldn't possibly, it's a common name. Why don't you describe it?"

"Well, my understanding is that it is a green crystalline object almost nine inches long, a sharp point at one end and rounded at the other. And it is cursed, deadly for anyone who covets it to possess it. It's said that hundreds have died for their trouble of stealing it. They die by being transformed into human statues of the same green crystal."

Michael noted that Luci's face drained of color as she listened to this odd story of religious arcana. He was fascinated by how ideas simply popped into existence without any antecedent and took on a robust life of their own; of course Olivia did report that she'd seen it with her own eyes. Maybe that is what disturbed Luci.

"What is it? Do you need something?" asked Michael.

"No, I'm fine."

"Good, then why don't we plan on dinner later?"

"That would be lovely," said Luci who was actually planning a trip.

Sonny and Spectre were on the Asylum grounds, a well placed bribe caused a security guard to forget to set the lock at the gate. They slipped in unobserved and using Joseph's map soon found their way to the cell Gaea had occupied since Fire dropped her into the grounds. As they made their way to the door a shouted command reached their ears.

"Stop them!" screamed Luci to the platoon of guardsmen she had hired for triple their daily wage at a local barroom.

As the guards tried to engage Sonny and Spectre Michael thundered into the corridor, swept past Luci and kicked down the door to Gaea's cell.

Spectre held Luci's minions at bay; the dog was a blur of claws and teeth. Blood splatter rained against the walls as they tried to land blows with cudgels, mauls and swords but the only damage inflicted was on themselves. It became apparent that Spectre was averse to giving a death strike as he limited himself to ankles and wrists but his teeth found their mark every time. The sound of battle abated as all the humans lay moaning on the floor unable to wield their weapons or even rise to their feet.

While Sonny confronted Luci, Michael ran to Gaea who slept on a spartan cot against the wall, even after thirty years her progress toward recovery was minimal. Tears streamed down his face as he held her against his chest. As she awoke a hint of a smile informed her mouth.

Sonny launched himself through the air with the intent of using a sissorslock around Luci's neck but halfway across the intervening distance he hit an invisible wall and crashed to the floor.

"Are you serious? Do you think you can lay hands on a Goddess? You show me no respect...I'm not only going to utterly destroy you, but it shall be done very slowly."

Luci advanced on Sonny's prostrate body. He appeared to have had the wind knocked out of him; he began to rise to his hands and knees.

Being an unquestioned unchallenged Goddess for over thirty years gave Luci a skewed idea of her power. She didn't give her opposition the respect they deserved -- being three demigods themselves. Having dispatched Luci's henchmen Spectre turned his attention to the self-described Goddess. His jaws slammed down on her right ankle with a crunch that would have sent a human into shock. But Luci screamed in rage rather than pain.

"You damn dog, once and for all I'm putting an end to you! I'm going skin you and stuff you, and leave you outside in the rain. You've been ...?"

She tried to whip the dog off her ankle by spinning on her other leg like a whirling dervish. Spectre hung tight. Michael gently propped Gaea up against the wall so she could see the conflict and threw himself into battle against Luci. He ran though a puddle of blood left by Spectre's attack and picked a maul out of the skull of one of Luci's retainers. He calmly stood judging the position of Luci's knee as she spun, when satisfied that he understood the geometry of her motion he pulled the maul up and from behind his head he swung it as hard as possible at Luci's knee, connecting with a sharp crack, sending her to the floor.

Sonny regained his equilibrium, tore the Dagger from the leather lattice at his neck and for the first time in his life laid eyes on his Mother, Gaea, the Living Goddess. He stood immobile, Gaea was still unable to even speak using her voice, but as Joseph could testify she could still communicate. Her voice was in Sonny's head.

"Sonny, you know the location of the mystical Third Eye?"

"Yes."

"Come to me, I will guide your hand. You must plunge the Dagger cleanly through my skull directly in my Third Eye."

"I can't hurt you."

"That's right, you can't, you won't, do it now!"

Sonny took her at her word and lunged at her putting all his strength into smashing the dagger into her head. There was almost no resistance and the crystal stopped with a half inch protruding like a medallion. The Dagger of God was casting an eerie green glow from Gaea's now visible third eye. The reintegration of the true Goddess with her missing essence was amazing to watch. A web of green lightening surrounded her from head to foot, throwing off sparks like a Roman candle; the aural effects were equally as impressive. The air temperature had risen significantly and the expansion of the air in the room caused a howl that would have been painful for human ears.

Sonny stood watching, in awe of his mother. Gaea was floating some six or seven feet off the floor. As the pyrotechnics subsided she slowly descended. She extended her arms to Sonny. They embraced. She pulled back to look at him.

"My son...what took you so long?" She asked, tousling his hair.

"Um, I had to find the "Dagger of God", it left quite a trail of corpses across the continent..."

"I'm teasing," Gaea said.

While the Goddess was demonstrably, once again, fully invested in her panoply of powers Luci was sprawled across the floor with her lower left leg jutting out at an impossible angle. Since there were only bone fragments in the ankle savaged by Spectre she did not have the ability to stand. Even a god such as herself needed time to rebuild extensive damage. Spectre took the opportunity to lightly close his jaws around Luci's neck.

"Michael, would you help her sit up? Luci, if you continue to struggle Spectre will separate your head from your shoulders. Your recovery would be long and quite boring, just nod if you agree."

Luci made a very small motion of her chin downward. Gaea waved her hand in Luci's direction, she was enveloped in yet another green glow and her wounds were quickly healed. Michael helped her to her feet. Spectre padded to his side.

"I will not continue this conversation with the simulacrum that stands before me, restore the form I originally gave you," ordered Gaea.

Luci's body began to ripple, her face broadened, lost its delicate oval aspect, her jaw thickened. She grew several inches and her breasts collapsed. Now Gaea looked upon a very chastened Fire, he would not return her gaze.

"Fire! No, Fire was a beautiful boy whom I loved with all the passion at my disposal. Your name is Lucifer the Usurper…"

"Luci told me that Fire went back into the world…I really thought the Goddess went in search of him, I feel so stupid," confessed Michael to all assembled.

"Michael, your heart can't even conceive of deception, I don't think less of you."

"I wish someone would explain everything to me! I'm at quite a disadvantage here. I've spent the last thirteen years wandering the deserts seeking the "Dagger of God" because a little voice in my head kept pushing me," said Sonny.

"That would be me, Sonny," said Gaea, "don't worry; I'll bring you up to date."

"Are you going to kill me?" Asked Lucifer.

"Don't be ridiculous, that would be far too light a punishment. In fact I think I will allow you to become my constant companion once again."

The look of terror that had inhabited Lucifer's face since Gaea had regained her place in the firmament suddenly was washed away by undeserved relief. He couldn't believe his luck.

"Oh my Goddess, thank you, thank you. I will spend the rest of my life paying my debt to you. Thank you."

"Of that, there can be no doubt," said Gaea, chuckling, and then laughing.

She proffered her two hands palms up, one to Spectre and one to Lucifer. The by now familiar green energy beams sprayed out and this time a loop between the two was formed. Spectre began to stretch his front and rear legs, his back rising in the air while the exact opposite was happening to Lucifer.

In a moment an extremely handsome man stood where Spectre had previously been licking his privates. His face was filled with pure wonderment. He looked afraid, or at least unable, to speak. Gaea, on the other hand, broke out in a broad smile aimed right at the handsome man.

Lucifer looked terrified, that was the lasting impression an observer would have taken away as the now former faux Goddess inhabited a body matching Spectre. The new dog began to howl in the most forlorn way. He was ignored.

"Husband! It's so nice to see you once again; tell me, are you well and truly sorry for having offended me?" Asked Gaea with a very pleased twinkle in her eye.

Paradise redux.

cookie crumbles

Miss Cookie Crumbles is a drag performer, writer, performance artist and a damn fine cook. She was born on the far side of the Cheddar Curtain but moved south during the Cretaceous Period. She lives in Chicagoland while waiting for Ragnarok. She enjoys frequent sojourns in New Orleans where she collects beads, doubloons, recipes, story ideas and viruses. Thanks to her association with Chicago's NewTown Writers she has had the opportunity to perform in many stage shows over the past eight years and looks forward to many more. She hopes if you enjoy this book you'll tell all your friends and if you don't she hopes you'll lie.